JUST DESSERTS

by
NORMA COLE and NANEKI ELLIOTT

Based on Eliza Calvert Hall's
Aunt Jane of Kentucky

Dramatic Publishing
Woodstock, Illinois • England • Australia • New Zealand

*** NOTICE ***

The amateur and stock acting rights to this work are controlled exclusively by THE DRAMATIC PUBLISHING COMPANY without whose permission in writing no performance of it may be given. Royalty fees are given in our current catalog and are subject to change without notice. Royalty must be paid every time a play is performed whether or not it is presented for profit and whether or not admission is charged. A play is performed any time it is acted before an audience. All inquiries concerning amateur and stock rights should be addressed to:

DRAMATIC PUBLISHING
P. O. Box 129, Woodstock, Illinois 60098

COPYRIGHT LAW GIVES THE AUTHOR OR THE AUTHOR'S AGENT *THE EXCLUSIVE RIGHT TO MAKE COPIES.* This law provides authors with a fair return for their creative efforts. Authors earn their living from the royalties they receive from book sales and from the performance of their work. Conscientious observance of copyright law is not only ethical, it encourages authors to continue their creative work. This work is fully protected by copyright. No alterations, deletions or substitutions may be made in the work without the prior written consent of the publisher. No part of this work may be reproduced or transmitted in any form or by any means, electronic or mechanical, including photocopy, recording, videotape, film, or any information storage and retrieval system, without permission in writing from the publisher. It may not be performed either by professionals or amateurs without payment of royalty. All rights, including but not limited to the professional, motion picture, radio, television, videotape, foreign language, tabloid, recitation, lecturing, publication and reading, are reserved.

For performance of any songs and recordings mentioned in this play which are in copyright, the permission of the copyright owners must be obtained or other songs and recordings in the public domain substituted.

©MM by
NORMA COLE and NANEKI ELLIOTT

Printed in the United States of America
All Rights Reserved
(JUST DESSERTS)

ISBN 1-58342-018-5

IMPORTANT BILLING AND CREDIT REQUIREMENTS

All producers of the play *must* give credit to the author(s) of the play in all programs distributed in connection with performances of the play and in all instances in which the title of the play appears for purposes of advertising, publicizing or otherwise exploiting the play and/or a production. The name of the author(s) *must* also appear on a separate line, on which no other name appears, immediately following the title, and *must* appear in size of type not less than fifty percent the size of the title type. Biographical information on the author(s), if included in this book, may be used on all programs. *On all programs this notice must appear:*

"Produced by special arrangement with
THE DRAMATIC PUBLISHING COMPANY of Woodstock, Illinois"

For Norma Cole

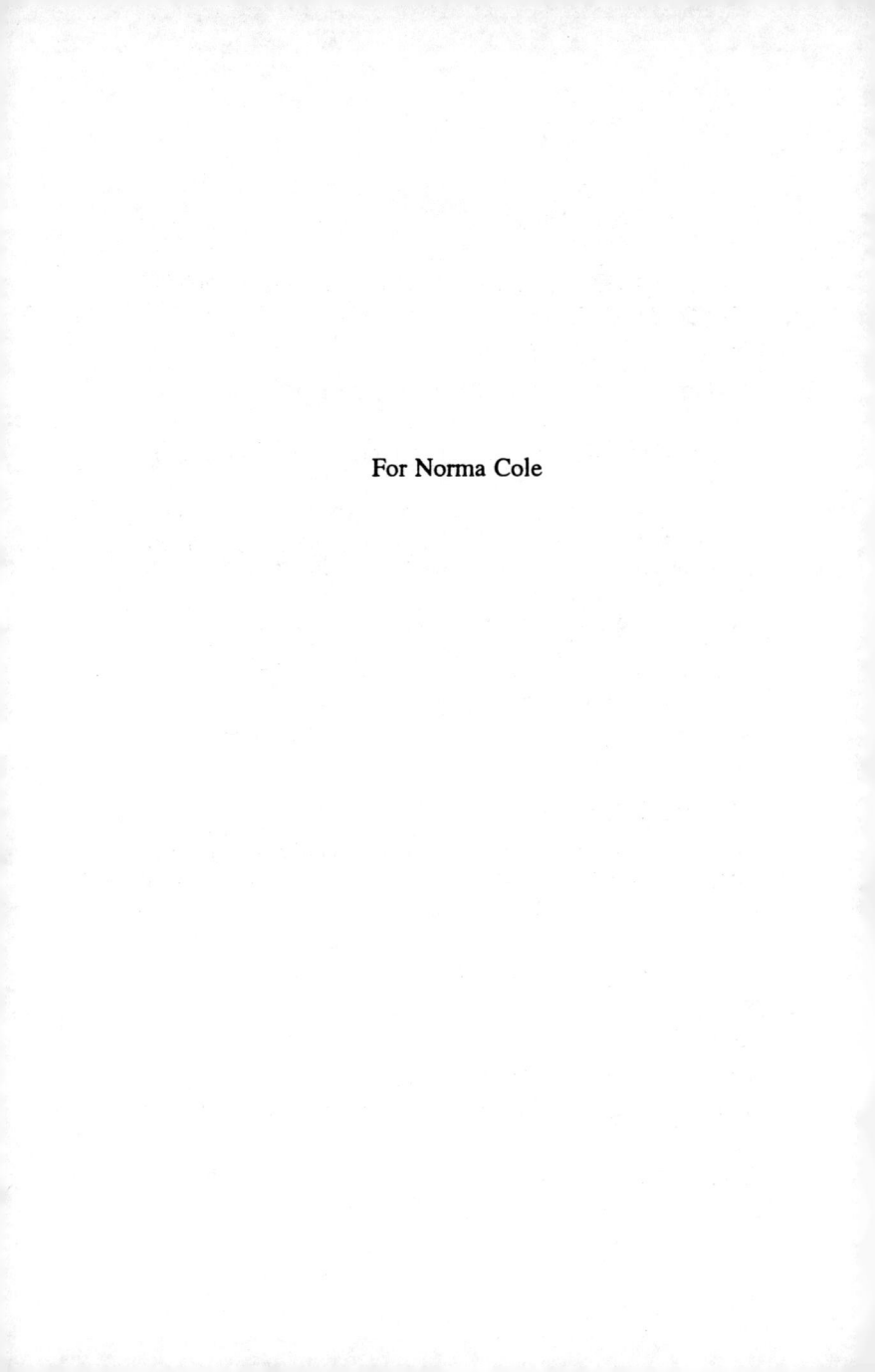

Just Desserts was first produced in play readings by the authors in 1996. Cole and Elliott took the play to schools, churches and other groups in rural areas of Kentucky. In January 1997, the play was awarded a grant for further work from the Kentucky Foundation for Women. *Just Desserts* was presented at the Women Writers' Conference at the University of Kentucky in October 1997. In March 1998, Pat Wetherton and Sylvia Bruton, actors from Louisville, began to perform the play at universities and various organizations in both Louisville and Lexington as well as in rural areas of the state.

JUST DESSERTS

A Play in One Act
For 2 Women

CHARACTERS

AUNT JANE: An elderly widow-woman.

SALLY ANN: also plays 'LIZABETH SPENCER,
MAYBELLE BUXTON, GERTIE EMBRY.

TIME and PLACE:

The play is set in a rural community in that amorphus time between the American Civil War and the turn of the 20th century.

Running time: 50 minutes

JUST DESSERTS

SET: *A rural home of the late 1800s. Two comfortable chairs with a tea table between reveals tea things and a large Bible. A small basket of quiltmaking cloth is near one chair and a knit shawl is visible. (Certain props will be needed to allow SALLY ANN to evoke the other women in the story.)*

AT RISE: *AUNT JANE wears garments suitable to the era and her station as a widow. She hums or sings the old hymn "Sweet Hour of Prayer." She becomes aware of the audience and speaks to them.*

AUNT JANE. Well, there you are. I see you found a chair. I reckon you must be a-wondering what I'm doing, widow-woman that I am, sitting alone in this old house. I'm reading my Bible some and fixing to make one more quilt. Oh, I know I said I was done with such work, but the Women's Mite Society of Goshen Church needs a quilt to raffle off and I think I'll get it started. *(She selects three pieces of quilt cloth to talk about.)* This piece was from my niece, Rebecca. My, she was a fine, young determined woman... This was of a dress I got the spring before Abram died... Now, Sally Ann Flint gave me this bit. Wasn't she a good'un? *(She holds up a long piece of purple cloth that shows where something has been cut out.)* Lookie here what I found. Sally Ann's suffragist banner was made from this. I wish I could have seen them brave women all dressed in white, wearing their purple banners so proud, marching for their rights... Did I ever tell you about Sally Ann's experience that put us women of Goshen Church to the mind that we could do something for ourselves? Well, it was forty year ago if it was a day. The way of it was this: The men of the church got the roof patched and put in a new window light. We women of the Mite Society begun talking about getting a carpet for the bare floor. Some of us wanted the carpet and some of us wanted to give the money to the foreign mission as we'd set out to do at the first. We got into quite a racket and it took Sally Ann Flint to settle the fuss.

(SALLY ANN enters. She is younger than AUNT JANE, dressed in a more decorative garment, and could have an outrageous hat.)

- SALLY ANN. Well, if any of the heathen fails to hear the gospel on account of us getting some carpet, they'll be saved anyway, so Brother Page says. If we send the money and they do hear the gospel, like as not they won't repent and then they're sure to be damned. It seems to me that as long as we don't know what they'll do, we might as well keep the money and get the carpet. I never did see much sense in giving folks a chance to damn theirselves. *(Exits.)*
- AUNT JANE. We began talking about appointing a committee to go to town the following Monday and pick out the carpet. All at once, 'Lizabeth Spencer, our treasurer, spoke up.

('LIZABETH enters.)

'LIZABETH. There ain't no use appointing that committee. I kept the money in the top bureau drawer and when I went for it yesterday, it was gone. I'll pay it back if I'm ever able, but I ain't able now. *(Exits.)*

AUNT JANE. Lizzy? Our 'Lizabeth? You suppose that husband of hers, Jacob, took our money? Brother Page's wife—she was as good a woman as ever lived—said just two words:... "Judge not." And then Sally Ann spoke up.

(SALLY ANN enters.)

SALLY ANN. For the Lord's sake, don't let the menfolks know anything about this. They're always saying that women ain't fit to handle money, and I don't want to give 'em any more ground to stand on then they think they've already got. *(Exits.)*

AUNT JANE. We agreed with Sally Ann... all but that Milly Amos. She had mite little sense to begin with and having been married about two months, she'd lost that little... 'cause I happened to meet her young husband, Sam, and he says to me, "Aunt Jane, how much money you women of the Mite Society got toward the carpet?" I looked him square on and I says, "Sam Amos, if you be a member of the Women's Mite Society of Goshen Church, you already know. And if you ain't, you got no business knowing." That settled him... Now, none of us saw 'Lizabeth outside her door for most of a month. Though many of us called on her, she told nary one her troubles until that prayer meeting night... We'd sung "Sweet Hour of Prayer," Brother Page prayed and then he called upon the brethren to tell of their experience with the Lord this past week. Old Uncle Jim Matthews cleared his throat. I knew as well as I know my name he was fixing to tell how precious the Lord had been...but before he got started, here come 'Lizabeth down the side aisle,

('LIZABETH enters.)

AUNT JANE *(cont'd).* and she stopped right in front of the pulpit.

'LIZABETH. I've something to say. It was me that took the missionary money we was to use for the carpet. I took it to pay my way to Louisville the time I got word that my dear daughter from my first marriage was dying. I asked Jacob three times for the money. When he refused, I tried to put it out of my mind and stay home. Finally, I said to myself, "I'm going anyway." As soon as Jacob had ate his breakfast and went out on the farm, I dressed myself. When I opened the top bureau drawer to get my best collar, I saw it...the missionary money. I tried not to think about keeping it, but the thought kept coming back. Getting Jacob's carpetbag, I happened to look up at the mantelpiece. I saw the candlesticks with prisms all around that my mamma had given me long, long ago. I knew just then what the Lord intended me to do... Some of you recollect I had a boarder summer before last...

AUNT JANE. That genealogy lady from Louisville.

'LIZABETH. That's right. She offered me fifteen dollar for the candlesticks. I wouldn't part with them, but she left her name and address on a card. I got that card out of the big Bible and packed them candlesticks in the carpetbag. After I put on my bonnet I went out to the gate. There was Dave Crawford coming along in his new buggy and he offered to take me to town... I got to Mary just two hours before she died. She looked up in my face and says, "Mamma, I knew God wouldn't let me die 'til I'd seen you once more." I believed the Lord was leading me all this time, but the way things turned out, it musta been Satan.

AUNT JANE. I can't hardly tell this without crying. 'Lizabeth talked straight on as if she'd made up her mind to say just so much, and she'd die if she didn't get to say it.

'LIZABETH. As soon as the funeral was over, I set out to find the lady that wanted them candlesticks. She was gone for a few days, but her niece said she was sure her aunt still wanted them and would send the money right off... If that lady'd only come back when her niece said, it would have turned out all right, but I reckon it's a judgment on me for meddling with the Lord's money. I've been a member of this church for twenty year, but, though the money come today, I figure you'll turn me out now. *(Holds out the check.)*

AUNT JANE. The poor thing stood there trembling and holding out the check as if she expected somebody to come and take it. Old Silas Petty was a-glowering at her from under his eyebrows. *('LIZABETH exits.)* I recollect thinking, "Oh, if only the Lord Jesus would just come in and take her part." And while we sat there like a passel of mutes, Sally Ann Flint got up and stood right by 'Lizabeth.

(SALLY ANN enters.)

AUNT JANE *(cont'd)*. Well, I felt so relieved. It popped into my head that we didn't need the Lord right now, Sally Ann would do just as good.

SALLY ANN. Where's that eight hundred dollar 'Lizabeth had when she married you, Jacob Spencer? Down in that ten-acre meadow lot and in that new barn you built last spring? A man that won't even give his wife some of her own money to go to her dying child is too mean to stay in a Christian church. Elders sure ain't changed much since Biblical times.

AUNT JANE. Old Deacon Petty rose up. "Brethren," says he, "this is awful! If this woman wants to give her religious experience, why, of course she can do so. But when it comes to a *woman* standing up in the house of the Lord and reviling an elder as this woman is doing, why I tremble for the Church of Christ. For don't the 'postle Paul say, 'Let your women keep silence in the church'?"

(During the following nine speeches by SALLY ANN, AUNT JANE may add an "Amen," "Yes, yes," "Aye," as suitable.)

SALLY ANN. The 'postle Paul has been dead ruther too long for me to be afraid of him. If he don't like what I'm saying, let him rise up from his grave in Corinthians or Ephesians or wherever he's buried and say so... I've got a message for the menfolks of this church and I'm going to deliver it, Paul or no Paul.

AUNT JANE. You're telling it true, Sally Ann.

SALLY ANN. As for you, Silas Petty, I ain't forgot the time I dropped in to see Maria one Saturday night. I found her washing out her flannel petticoat and drying it before the fire. Ever time I've had to hear you lead in prayer, I've said to myself, "Lord, how high can a man's prayers rise toward heaven when his wife ain't got but one flannel skirt to her name?" No higher than the back of that pew, Silas Petty.

AUNT JANE. Job Taylor was a-setting right in front of Deacon Petty. I reckon he thought his time had come so he gets up, easy-like, and starts to sneak to the back door.

SALLY ANN. You come back here, Job Taylor. You set right down and hear what I've got to say. I've knelt and stood through enough of your long-winded prayers. Now it's my time to talk and yours to listen.

AUNT JANE. And bless your life if Job Taylor didn't set down, meek as Moses.

SALLY ANN. The only thing that stands in my way of telling some of your meanness is that there's so much to tell I don't know where to begin... We women know how Marthy scrimped and saved her egg money to buy a new set of furniture, how you took her money with you that time you went to Cincinnati the spring before Marthy died. You come back without the furniture... and when she asked about the money you said that everything she had belonged to you and that your mother's old furniture was good enough for anybody.

AUNT JANE. And nobody knew where the money went.

SALLY ANN. It's my belief that's what killed Marthy. Women are dying ever day. The doctors will tell you it's some new-fangled disease or other, when, if the truth was known, it's nothing but wanting something they can't get and hoping and waiting for something that never comes. I've watched 'em and I know... and furthermore, Job Taylor, where were you when your own sister, Gertie Embry, had to cut up her wedding skirts to make gowns and didies for that first baby? Did you step in to help that young pair? Knowing how things are with Gertie these days, I think not.

AUNT JANE. Job sat there looking like a sheep-killing dog. I heard Dave Crawford shuffling his feet and clearing his throat. Dave come up against Sally Ann in a lawsuit one time and he lost. He's been calling her a "he-woman" ever since.

SALLY ANN. Do you think your scraping and hemming is going to stop me, Dave Crawford? You've been known to be generous... but most of the time you're one of the men that makes me think it's better to be a Kentucky horse than a Kentucky woman... Many's the day I've seen your poor wife, her head tied up, crawling around trying to cook for sixteen harvest hands and you out in the stable rubbing down your three-year-olds to get 'em ready for the fair... It's mighty hard to understand how a man can have more mercy on his horse than to the woman he married. July's found rest at last out in the graveyard and ever time I pass your house I thank the Lord that you got to pay a good price for your cooking now as there ain't a woman in the county fool enough to step into July's shoes.

AUNT JANE. Sally Ann had her say about nearly ever man in the church. Just as I was a-wondering if she was going to let the minister off, she began...

SALLY ANN. Brother Page, you're a good man, but you ain't so good you couldn't be better. When it comes to the perseverance of the saints and the decrees of God, there ain't many can preach a better sermon than you. But there's some of your sermons that ain't fit for much but...

SALLY ANN & AUNT JANE. ...kindling fires...

SALLY ANN. You've been expounding on the fifth chapter of Ephesians. I believe we've men in this church that thinks the fifth chapter of Ephesians ain't got but twenty-four verses, so I'm going to remind you about the rest of that...

AUNT JANE *(holds up her Bible; cuts in)*. Psst, Sally Ann. Show 'em the big gun.

SALLY ANN *(recognizes AUNT JANE with a nod)*. Husbands, love your wives even as Christ also loved the church and gave himself for it... Now I'm going to read the twenty-eighth verse so there's no doubt what the good Lord meant... "So ought men to love their wives as their own bodies... He that loveth his wife loveth himself..." If I had the preaching to do, I'd say that when Paul told women to be subject to their husbands in everthing, he wasn't inspired. When he told men to love their wives as Christ loved the church, he was filled with the holy spirit! As for turning 'Lizabeth out of the church, I'd like to know who's to do the turning out. If there's a man today good enough to set in judgment on a woman, his name ain't on the roles of Goshen Church. Besides, the matter of that money don't concern nobody but our Mite Society. We women can settle it without any help from you deacons and elders.

AUNT JANE. I could see Brother Page thinking he better head Sally Ann off some way so he calls out, "Let's sing...everbody...'Blest Be the Tie That Binds.' " About the middle of the first verse, Miz Page got up and went over to 'Lizabeth and give her the right hand of fellowship. Then Miz Petty done the same and the first thing we knew we was all 'round Lizzy shaking hands and hugging her and crying over her... *(SALLY ANN exits.)* God bless you, Lizzy... 'Twas a regular love-feast, and we went home feeling like we'd been through a big protracted meeting and got religion all over again... I've thought many a time that Sally Ann's plain talk done more good than all the sermons us women has had preached to us about being shamefaced and submitting to our husbands. Most of us women came out with new dresses and bonnets that spring... You might be a-wondering about Abram—and me. Didn't Sally Ann have nothing to say about us in her experience? La, no. Abram never was that kind of a man and I never was that kind of a woman... I recollect as we was walking home that prayer-meeting night, Abram says, sort of humble-like, "Jane, hadn't you better get that brown merino cloth you was a-looking at last county court day?" And I says, "Don't you worry about that brown merino cloth, Abram. It's a-lying in my bottom drawer right now. I told the storekeeper to cut it off just as soon as your back was turned..." Abram says, "Well, Jane, I never saw the beat of you." *(AUNT JANE finds a knit shawl and puts it in her lap or on her shoulders.)* I've noticed that whenever a woman's willing to be imposed on, there's always a man standing around ready to do the imposing. You remember how them property laws used to be? Why, a woman could work all her married life and end up with nothing more than a third if her husband died... if she died, he got it all! Things is different from what they used to be. Richard Baker—Julie's boy?—he turned out to be a fine lawyer. He went with that passel of women to Frankfort and so pestered the legislature that those men had to change the property

JUST DESSERTS

laws just to get rid of them determined women... Speaking of Richard Baker—I knit this shawl for his mamma long about the time she took sick. Some say it was the consumption, and I reckon it was... All this reminds me of the time Richard's daddy come back here... Lordy! He'd been gone all of twenty year. I can see it plain as day the morning Maybelle Buxton—that young hired girl?—she come along just after sunrise...

(MAYBELLE enters, breathless.)

MAYBELLE. Jane! Jane! You won't believe what I saw last night over at old Squire Elrod's.

AUNT JANE. Now, Maybelle, First Timothy 5:13 tells us women not to be idle, wandering about from house to house, and not only idle, but gossips and busybodies saying things we ought not.

MAYBELLE. Then I'm not to tell you?

AUNT JANE. I didn't say that.

MAYBELLE. I swear to God it's the truth.

AUNT JANE. There's no need to be swearing on God. He hears enough of that. If it's not gossip, tell me what you seen...

MAYBELLE. Dick Elrod's come back to his daddy. Old Squire Elrod took him in.

AUNT JANE. Dick Elrod's come home? That scoundrel. Why, I thought he'd disappeared forever. After what he did to ruin the lives of two young women, I'd as soon not see his face again.

MAYBELLE. I reckon you won't have to. He looked so poorly last night the doctor told the old squire he didn't think Dick had long to live.

AUNT JANE. Most probably he lived his life the way he started out, drinking and carousing. Such living soon leaves a body spent. *(MAYBELLE is hopping around.)* What you hopping around for? If you got more to tell, set right down and calm yourself.

MAYBELLE. You know that young student preacher at Goshen Church—Brother Jonas? He was there, too.

AUNT JANE. What? Why didn't you tell me before?

MAYBELLE. You was talking.

AUNT JANE. I know I was a-talking. Talking's one of the things I do best. If you've got something important to say, just interrupt me—

MAYBELLE *(cuts in)*. I'll try—

AUNT JANE *(cuts in)*. —whether I'm your elder or not.

MAYBELLE. Well, Brother Jonas must have gotten wind of Dick's homecoming right off 'cause he come to the squire's house last night fixing to convert him.

AUNT JANE. I expect he thought it would be a feather in his cap if he could convert a hardened old sinner like Dick Elrod.

MAYBELLE. The preacher went into Dick's room and sat down on the bed and began to lay off the plan of salvation just like he was preaching from the pulpit.

AUNT JANE. I can't quite see Dick Elrod taking that in—

MAYBELLE *(cuts in)*. He listened, all right. Never took his eyes off the brother's face. But when the brother finished, Dick says, "Do you mean to say that all I've got to do to get into heaven is to believe on the Lord Jesus Christ?" and Brother Jonas says, "Believe on the Lord Jesus Christ and thou shalt be saved. The blood of Jesus Christ, his son, cleanseth us from all sin."

AUNT JANE. What'd Dick Elrod have to say to that?

MAYBELLE. Oh my, he just laughed a curious sort of laugh and says, "It's a pretty God that'll make such a bargain as that... I was born bad, I've lived bad and I'm dying bad, but I ain't a coward nor a sneak and I'm going to hell for my sins like a man... Like a man, do you hear me?" The look in his eyes was awful, Jane, and the preacher turned white as a sheet.

AUNT JANE. It's mighty odd talk for a sick man, but, when you come to think about it, it's reasonable enough. When a man's got hell in his heart, what good is it going to do him to get to heaven?

MAYBELLE. I don't know... The preacher got up to go. Dick called him back and says, "I don't want any of your preaching or praying at my funeral, but you stay here, there's another sort of job to do"... He turned to his father and says, "Send for Julie."

AUNT JANE. He sent for Julie? What about her boy, Richard? How was Julie going to tell him? None of us has ever said a word. Richard was too decent a child and now a man to think he wasn't born as good as the rest of us.

MAYBELLE. When Julie come into the room, Dick gave a start. I reckon he expected to see the same young girl he'd fooled twenty year back. "Julie," he says, "I want to marry you. Don't refuse me. I want to do one decent thing before I die. I've come all the way from California just for this. Surely you'll feel better if you are my lawful wife."

AUNT JANE. Lordy, Lordy. Imagine him begging like that.

MAYBELLE. She says, "Dick, I've learned to live without that honor."

AUNT JANE. No.

MAYBELLE. Yes! He narrowed his eyes and says, "I know I was a cheat and a liar, Julie. I was a boy who thought I could have everything. I want to make things right for you and my son." Julie stands straight as an arrow and says, "Making things right don't matter to me no more. Richard and I have lived all right on what little I earn and what Richard earns from working here on the farm for your daddy."

AUNT JANE. My goodness, I am proud of Julie talking to him thataway. She doesn't owe nobody nothing, especially that scoundrel, Dick Elrod.

MAYBELLE. Oh, I don't know, Jane. I felt right sorry for him. He wouldn't give up. He says, "You owe me nothing, Julie, but think of Richard. If we marry, you'll have money to set him up right comfortable on a farm of his own. I squandered a lot of money out West, but there's plenty left."

AUNT JANE. That man! He's as much as bribing her. What a shameful thing to do to an honest woman.

MAYBELLE. I think he was trying to make up for bad times.

AUNT JANE. I don't believe you knowed him like I did. You were but a child when he was a-tearing around here, sowing his wild oats... but, go on... Did Julie accept?

MAYBELLE. She excused herself. "I'm going to speak to Richard in the parlor," she says. Well, I had to hear what she was telling him, so I left the room and listened and looked through the keyhole.

AUNT JANE. Not good practice, Maybelle... but... What did you...?

MAYBELLE. Julie was forward with Richard and told him everything that had been said. When she finished, he says, "Mother, you have no obligation to marry that man. The money doesn't matter. I can earn good wages right here or anywhere else."

AUNT JANE *(whoops).* What a boy! A mamma's pride and joy!

MAYBELLE. But that's not all. Julie says, "The only thing that's hard to earn is a college education. If you be wanting something like that, son, then I'd be willing to marry him."

AUNT JANE. Oh, my. That must have been hard for her to say.

MAYBELLE. It was. Julie was near to tears. I could hear Richard shuffling his feet sometime before he says, "I promise you, Mother, if I do get to go to college on this man's money, I'll become a lawyer and try to change things for women. It ain't right for a woman to have to marry a man she doesn't want so her son can get his rightful share." When Dick saw Richard, he raised up on his elbow, weak as he was and he hollered out, "Why, it's myself! Stand off there, where I can see you, boy! You'll be the man I ought to have been and couldn't be. These lying doctors tell me I haven't got long to live, but I'm going to live another lifetime in you."

AUNT JANE. No.

MAYBELLE. Yes!

AUNT JANE. And?

MAYBELLE. Richard stood there solemn as a preacher while Julie says, "I'll marry you, Dick, but it's only for the benefit of my son." Then Dick says, "That's enough reason for me." And he opened his hand. "I took this ring away from you twenty year ago, Julie, for fear you'd use it against me, scoundrel that I was. Now I'm going to put it back on your finger and the parson here shall marry us fair and square. I've got the license here under my pillow."

AUNT JANE. Oh, envy's not something to be proud of, but I got a bit in my heart right now for you having been there and not me.

MAYBELLE. Julie says, "I don't need no ring for proof, Dick Elrod, but I'll wear it until you die." Then Brother Jonas said the ceremony over 'em. Oh, I had a hard time keeping back my tears. All this long, long time and he only now come to his senses.

AUNT JANE. Now, don't get to flooding this place before the story's told... I believe there is more to tell?

MAYBELLE. Oh, there is. Julie went to Richard and laid her hand on his arm and says, "My son, come and speak to your father"... Dick hung on to his son's hand... Then he reached under his pillow and brought out a paper and he says, "It's my will. Open it after I'm gone. I've left you and your mother plenty to live on and that mining stock will make you a rich man. I wish it was more, for you are a son that a king'd be proud of"... Them was about the last words he said. Dr. Pendleton said Dick might not live through the night and sure enough, he begun to sink as soon as the young brother left. He died about daybreak.

AUNT JANE. Dick come and gone so quick and Julie and Richard there with him. To live to hear of such a day.

MAYBELLE. When I left, they was laying out the body. And I saw, as Julie shut the door behind me, that she wasn't wearing that ring. *(MAYBELLE exits.)*

AUNT JANE *(to audience)*. God love her. Maybelle was a simple soul. Now, this life don't got to be a vale of tears unless you make it so on purpose. Of all the satisfactions

I ever experienced, the most satisfying is to see people get their just desserts right here in this world. *(She takes a few beats to find the purple cloth and a special teacup.)* Lookie here! Ever time I see this cup I think of Mary Clark and that first man of hers, Harvey Andrews. He tried to rule Mary with a short rein and a hard bit the way you'd break a feisty mare, him not seeing her as a woman who'd need a gentle, loving hand. You recollect that dinner party? I reckon Gertie Embry never had forgot that particular occasion. Gertie was already a widow-woman of an advanced age...not that she'd ever told, but she was considerable older than me! Bless her heart, she had to do hired-girl work up to nearly when she died, her being left with nothing but debts by her man.

(GERTIE enters.)

GERTIE. That Sally Ann Flint! What she said about me that prayer meeting night! I was glad to cut up my wedding skirts for my baby's gowns and didies. Me and my young husband was a-doing the best we could and he didn't deserve me doing nothing but my part. In my house he made the decisions and he had the last word... 'pears to me, this old world would be a sight better if things was still thataway...

AUNT JANE. Ain't you here to talk about that dinner party?

GERTIE. You know what First Timothy 5:13 says about widow women? It says we—

AUNT JANE *(cuts in)*. I can quote my Bible as much as you, Gertie Embry, so don't be trying to shame me out of this story. Are you going to tell it or not?

GERTIE. I will! I will! I ain't got nothing against Mary Andrews... her man, Harvey, was a miser and of a jealous nature, but I believe Sally Ann Flint went too far with her preaching to Mary about women's voting and getting into politicking...

AUNT JANE. You ain't said yet that Mary and Harvey was to entertain Harvey's cousin, old Judge McGowan from Tennessee, and how Harvey had hired you to help Mary put on that dinner party. I recollect how you always begun telling this story by saying, "That pair was so pretty..."

GERTIE. Kitty? Why you talking about cats? Harvey Andrews wouldn't have one on the place. He always said cats was the devil incarnate.

AUNT JANE *(to audience)*. I'd say he was the one to know. *(Raises her voice.)* I wasn't talking about cats. I said you said Mary and Harvey was such a pretty pair, tall and personable, both of...

GERTIE. I can hear you, Jane, so don't be a-yelling at me. If you'd just quit that mumbling...

AUNT JANE. Well, it wasn't long before we knew things wasn't so pretty between them. I had an idea that trouble was a-brewing the day them newlyweds had Abram and me over for our return dinner. Mary's daddy, old Jerry Clark, had set them up in a nice house. Lordy, he was the freest man I ever knowed. He held with the Kentuckians Eleventh Commandment: "Do not neglect the stranger at the door." He always laughed when he said, "If you are at my door..."

AUNT JANE & GERTIE *(mingle voices)*. "... you ain't a stranger."

GERTIE. In my opinion he was too free by half. Mary was her father's own daughter and look what being thataway did for her.

AUNT JANE. Mary must've found it hard that Harvey was—well—like he was. He was honest and industrious and had his farm all paid for, but he was of a different mold as Abram and me begun to see that day we was there. Mary was a-showing us around her new house after dinner, and we come upon Harvey leaning over the dining table a-counting out the silver spoons... And Mary says to him, "Oh, Harvey, not the spoons"... Later on I thought I seen him slip them spoons into his pocket.

GERTIE. Why, I stand amazed.

AUNT JANE. I guess... Poor Mary's face turned red right up to the roots of her hair. That night I asked Abram if he ever had cause to think that Harvey was a close man. Abram says, "Why, no. He looks after his own interests in a trade, but he is a liberal giver to Goshen Church. Besides," he says, "whoever heard of a tall personable man like Harvey Andrews being a miser. Stingy people are always dried up and shriveled-looking. Take you, Jane, you'll never make a miser, you being a woman pleasingly plump."

GERTIE. That dinner party proved how wrong your Abram was about Harvey.

AUNT JANE. The day was fixed with the judge coming up to Kentucky for that politicking our men were so hot about. Harvey declared he would have his cousin set at his table and eat his dinner 'stead of staying at the pig roast the men was to have in town. Some didn't like the plan, but that was that, Harvey said. And that was the way it was.

GERTIE. You recollect Mary had some plans, too? When I went over that morning bright and early, there was Mary setting on the porch sewing. The house was cleaned up. I saw a pan of fresh garden greens on the table but not a sign of company dinner to be seen. Mary liked to have knocked me over with a feather when she told me to sit down and rest myself. Finally I says, "Mary, I ain't the fast worker I used to be and a company dinner ain't a small thing to fix. Don't you think it's time to begin?" Mary answers, as calm as can be, "It don't take long for greens and cornbread to cook."

AUNT JANE. Greens and cornbread sure ain't a company dinner in my book!

GERTIE. Book? You saying cookbook? I don't need no receipt book to fix greens...

AUNT JANE. Now, Gertie, just go on and tell it straight out...nobody said nothing about your cooking.

GERTIE. I'm a good bit older'n you are, Jane Parrish, and I been a-cooking forever.

AUNT JANE. Aye, it is a woman's lifetime work. But, Gertie, what about that particular dinner?

GERTIE. When Mary told me to get started I walked into the pantry and there was the vittles Harvey had told me he was planning to have. I could hardly keep my hands off the ham, but I did smuggle out a few potatoes to boil.

AUNT JANE. You must have been plumb flummoxed.

GERTIE. I was, but I had my orders and fixed what she named. After Harvey had brought the judge around he took the horse to the barn and stopped by the kitchen to check on the dinner. Just then Mary come to see how I was a-doing. Harvey whirled on his wife and says, "Where is the ham and victuals you was told to fix? What is the meaning of this?" Mary just straight out says, "This means, Harvey, that what is good enough for your family is good enough for your kin."

AUNT JANE. I can't think of many new-married women would say something like that.

GERTIE. Oh, the look that passed between the two of them! Then Harvey says, sort of hard and flat-like, "It's them meetings you've been going to, turning your head around. I forbade you going with that Sally Ann Flint"... Mary held her ground. "It ain't the meetings, Harvey, this is between you and me"... Harvey didn't have nothing to say to that... Then he spun around and stalked out of the house. Mary told the judge that Harvey had some farm work to do, but Harvey did not come in the whole of the meal.

AUNT JANE *(to audience)*. Then Gertie told me something she said she hadn't told no one else.

GERTIE. Jane? You ever notice that little old shed-sort of a building on that farm? On down beyond the spring house?

AUNT JANE. I sure hadn't before that dinner, but I sure did after that.

GERTIE. The way those rafters slanted made it look shacky and rotting, windows all boarded up... I reckon I noticed it that day on account of the tin roof shining in the sun... I says to myself, that must be a little crib where Harvey keeps corn nubs for his horse... Well, while Mary was a-taking the judge to town to the train, I finished cleaning up the kitchen and closed up the house.

As I was a-crossing the yard I seen Harvey come out of the house with something in his arms. He went toward that little shed...and it looked like he had that pretty gold mantel clock Mary's mamma had given to her. I almost called goodbye to him, but he stopped in front of that shed and just stood there, stiff-like—face turned away... So I didn't say nothing. He looked right spooky, as if he meant to stand there 'til Judgment Day.

AUNT JANE. Knowing what we know now, I'd say judgment had already fallen on him.

GERTIE. I'd say so...such a shame, a dern shame.

AUNT JANE. Odd, you seeing him standing by that shed like that. I recollect I was home when the bad news come. Abram was a-telling me about the politicking when we heard horses moving mighty fast along the pike. We rushed to the front gate just in time to see Sam Amos pull up. He calls out, "Abram, Harvey Andrews has had an apoplexy fit. Go get the undertaker."

GERTIE. Gone. Just like that. And not another word between him and Mary.

AUNT JANE. I reckon Mary found him when she come home.

GERTIE. What a shock, and Mary having a young'un to raise on her own. If she'd been a proper wife and done what she was told, things woulda been different. That Sally Ann Flint... *(Exits.)*

AUNT JANE *(to audience).* Even after all these years, Gertie ain't heard all of that story. I'd promised Mary I'd never tell and I hadn't told. Wasn't I flummoxed when Sally Ann let it slip that she had known Mary's secret! We'd been talking about Harvey Andrews...he died about a year or so after Sally Ann come home from that

JUST DESSERTS

Beaumont Ladies Academy where they tried to make a lady out of her. Early on, Sally Ann's daddy thought Harvey'd be a good match for her. Lordy, putting Harvey Andrews with Sally Ann woulda been like lighting fire to dinny-mite*.

(SALLY ANN enters.)

SALLY ANN. I didn't think Harvey and Mary were suitable, but I gave 'em my blessing, happy in my heart I wasn't to be the bride.

AUNT JANE. If you suspected something then, couldn't you have warned her?

SALLY ANN. I tried, but you can't warn no one, even your best friend, if they've got their mind set. Besides, nobody really knew about Harvey until after... you remember how miserly he turned out, and how jealous? He was from Tennessee and hadn't been in the neighborhood long enough for anyone to get to know his ways. You recollect his funeral?

AUNT JANE. Mary was in a bad way. She couldn't seem to cry or talk or rest. As I was a-fastening on her crepe collar she says to me, "I reckon you think it's strange that I don't cry or take on like women do when they lose their husbands? You wouldn't blame me if you knew the truth." She dropped her voice to a whisper and she says, "I married Harvey Andrews, but after I married I found out he wasn't the man I thought he was. I don't know what's worse, to be sorry when I should be glad or glad

---
* dinny-mite = dynamite

when I should be sorry." I hushed her. Though I understood, there's some around here who wouldn'ta.

SALLY ANN. If she'd only listened to me.

AUNT JANE. The next day I found her with Harvey's things all about. She directed me to help pack a trunk and we pushed it up into the attic. As she was picking up a pile of clothes for the foreign missions, a key fell out of Harvey's pocket. Mary looked at it a long time, then she says, "Have you noticed things missing from this house? Ever time I've displeased Harvey he has taken something away from me..."

SALLY ANN. I knew all about that...I was there the night of the fire.

AUNT JANE. And how is it that you were there when me and the men from the fire brigade come?

SALLY ANN. The way of it was this: I had gone to a suffragist meeting with some of the women and Richard Baker...he was doing just what he'd told his mamma he would, helping women get our rights...

AUNT JANE. Stop your wandering off the story, Sally Ann.

SALLY ANN. I'm trying to tell you. Mary had been going to the meetings with me. Harvey didn't like that, I can tell it now. He made life miserable for her, demanding that she get over that nonsense. He said I was a bad influence on her...and I reckon I was. At least, I tried to be. Mary would have gone with me that night, but it being right after the funeral she thought to stay home. So, I was coming along the pike and I said to myself, if Mary has a light I'll take a chance that the baby will be asleep and maybe get a word or two with Mary. Mary had light all right. She was out in the yard with a torch.

AUNT JANE. A torch?

SALLY ANN. When she saw me she screamed and screamed. "I thought you was him. I thought you was him." "Harvey?" I says. "Harvey back from the dead?" "Three times he's been back to the shed," she says. "I had to do it. Don't you see what he wants?" I smelled smoke and I saw flames licking at a corner of that little shed. "Run, Mary, run!" I yelled. "Get some buckets"... Mary grabbed my hand in a grip of iron and she says, "Don't worry, Sally Ann. He wants my things; my silver spoons, my clock, my wedding dress, little Harvey's christening gown... I reckon he wants me and the baby. Well, he can have his plunder in the fires of hell, but never, never shall he take me or the child—"

AUNT JANE *(cuts in)*. I saw you a-holding Mary and she was a-crying as though her heart was broke. That little building burned to the ground and *now* I'd say it was right it did.

SALLY ANN. Mary got hold of things after that cry. But we soon learned that Harvey had the last word. He left that farm to his brother and only put aside a wee bit for little Harvey to have later on. Mary only got her third by law. Some time later she met a man from Louisville and moved away. I saw her now and then as the property rights folks kept at it 'til we won our fight. Mary has since gone on to other suffragist work. I expect I'll see her at the next Woman's Club meeting.

AUNT JANE. What you women pestering the legislature about now?

SALLY ANN. We're still trying to get the vote. You could help us out, you know.

(DIRECTOR'S NOTE: If you are planning to perform this piece for younger than a teenage audience, consider the alternate ending on page 35 in place of the following.)

(AUNT JANE chuckles and laughs.)

SALLY ANN *(cont'd)*. Now, Jane, what's so funny about you doing your part, too?

AUNT JANE. I'd think they was a-doing me like Abram said they did with Uncle Billy.

SALLY ANN. I don't follow your thinking.

AUNT JANE. Abram always said if they wanted to get shed of a nuisance around here they'd send him to the legislature...maybe sending me on a march would be the same—

SALLY ANN *(cuts her off)*. Humphh. I can't think how you'd compare yourself to that old reprobate. And he's been sent to the legislature twice.

AUNT JANE. I recollect the time Uncle Billy says, "Jane, I've been to Sodom and Gomorrah." So says I, "That's about the hardest thing I ever heard about a Kentucky legislature, and I've heard some pretty hard things in my day and time." And he says, "No, Jane, I ain't talking about the legislature; the legislature is all right. It's the women. The women, I tell you!"

SALLY ANN. That man's got the devil in his heart talking like that.

AUNT JANE. Says he, "There was a time when it was of some pleasure for a man to go up to the legislature. Us men, we'd get together and resolute, and debate, and pass our bills and everthing was as smooth as satin. Now and then we might get a letter from the homefolks about something that didn't suit 'em, but they was too far away to

JUST DESSERTS

worry us. But now I'd as soon as stay down on my farm if it wasn't for the money and the honor of the thing. The way it is now you got to wrastle with a lot of women that's strayed so far from the footsteps of their mothers and grandmothers...

SALLY ANN. We'd all be better off if he'd stayed to home on his farm. His mother and grandmother! Uncle Billy can't talk twenty minutes without telling how his mother had fifteen children, and she cooked and sewed and washed and ironed for 'em all, and how his grandmother fought a wildcat one night when her husband wasn't to home. That kind of life might have seemed like the Garden of Eden to Uncle Billy, but I'd like to know what his mother and grandmother thought. It don't sound like a bed of roses to me.

AUNT JANE. You're telling it true, Sally Ann! Well, Uncle Billy just talked on. He says, "I got so undone with them women that whenever a bill would come up, I'd say to whoever sat by me, 'Has the women got anything to do with this?' And if they did, I'd vote against it. If they hadn't, I'd vote for it, 'cause the more you give a woman the more she wants. We give them their property rights and now they're wanting to vote! I heard they want to run the schools and asylums and pretty near everthing else. There's women up there that don't know a water bucket from a churn, and if you was to show 'em a potater patch in full bloom they'd think it was some kind of a flower garden."

SALLY ANN. It'll be a glorious day when we women don't have to know just cooking and gardening. If I got anything to say about it, we'll be debating and passing bills in the legislature same as the menfolks... Jane, why don't you come with us to the next meeting? We're planning another march.

AUNT JANE. Folks would say I was too old for such carrying on, and I'd have to agree.

SALLY ANN. You know your heart's always been with us suffragists. Come on, now. We women need all the foot soldiers we can muster.

AUNT JANE. Honey, my feet's too tired for marching.

SALLY ANN. You don't need to march. Women are raising money, writing letters to the Uncle Billies of the Legislature...and talking. You know you're a good talker. Will you think about it?

AUNT JANE. I don't suppose you'll ever let me rest 'til I do. Now go on with you, Sally Ann.

SALLY ANN. All right! All right! *(Exits on next line.)* See you, Jane.

AUNT JANE. Sometimes I wish I had gone a-marching with them brave women. But, I have to face facts. I'm too old for such a thing now. *(She puts the purple cloth across her chest from shoulder to waist and poses here and there with it.)* Listen to my old talk. We women still ain't got that vote. *(She puts down the purple and lays some of the quilt pieces across the back of the chair.)* Well, I can piece this here quilt in a hurry...*and* I can tell the Mite Society that the money is to send some woman a-marching. *Then* I'm going to make me one of them banners and I'm going on that march. I don't care if folks poke fun at me the way we did Uncle Billy. I can help women get our just desserts and I wouldn't be surprised if the men would get theirs, too. *(She puts a piece of cloth over the back of the chair.)* Let's see now. I'll begin with this piece that was Rebecca's and this bit that was Sally Ann's. I wonder what else I got around here. Ain't I recollecting some brown goods down there in my bottom drawer... some brown merino cloth... Abram would like that. *(She laughs and begins her exit.)* He'd say, "Why, Jane, I never saw the beat of you."

THE END

* * * *

ALTERNATE ENDING (insert on page 32)

SALLY ANN *(cont'd).* Jane, why don't you come with us to the next meeting? We're planning another march.

AUNT JANE. They'd say I was too old for such carrying on, and I'd have to agree.

SALLY ANN. You know your heart's always been with us suffragists. Come on, now. We women need all the foot soldiers we can muster.

AUNT JANE. Honey, my feet's too tired for marching.

SALLY ANN. You don't need to march. Women are raising money, writing letters to the men of the legislature... and talking. You know you are a good talker. Will you think about it?

AUNT JANE. I don't suppose you'll ever let me rest 'til I do. Now, go on with you, Sally Ann. I got my work cut out for me.

SALLY ANN. All right! All right! *(Exits on next line.)* See you, Jane.

AUNT JANE. Sometimes I wish I had gone a-marching with them brave women. But I have to face facts. I'm too old for such a thing now. *(She puts the purple cloth across her chest from shoulder to waist. She poses around with it.)* Listen to my old talk. We women still ain't got the vote. *(She puts down the purple and shakes out a few pieces of the quilt cloth.)* Well, I can piece this here quilt in a hurry ... and I can tell the Mite Society that the money it brings in is to send some woman a-marching. And I'm going to make me one of them purple banners and ... I might just go on that march. I don't care if folks poke fun at me. I can help women get our just desserts and I wouldn't be surprised if the men would get theirs, too. *(She spreads more cloth around.)* Let's see. I think I'll begin with this piece that was Rebecca's and this piece that was Sally Ann's. I wonder what else I got around here. Ain't I recollecting some brown goods down there in my bottom drawer? Some brown merino cloth ... Abram would like that. *(She laughs on exit line.)* He'd say, "Jane, I never saw the beat of you!"

* * * *

A TRIBUTE TO NORMA COLE
by Naneki Elliott

(SALLY ANN sits in AUNT JANE's rocker in AUNT JANE's home. She rocks gently and hums "The Tie That Binds." She picks up AUNT JANE's sewing basket, picks out the plaid from her old skirt and also the bit of material for the suffragist banners that AUNT JANE had sewn. Hearing what she thinks is a gentle knock, she speaks.)

SALLY ANN. Come in. *(When no one enters, she looks around the room, stands up and pokes around the place. Thinking she hears someone again, she turns around.)* Come... Aunt Jane? Aunt Jane, is that you? *(There is a little giggle.)* Now, lookie here. If you're about this old place, let me know. Give me a sign.

(The old rocker begins to slowly rock and we can make out the figure of AUNT JANE standing behind it.)

Are you going to speak to me, or are you going to hang around giggling like some schoolgirl?

AUNT JANE. Don't be a-bothering me in my musings.
SALLY ANN. Who's bothering who? I didn't ask you to come.
AUNT JANE. Far as I know, you're the visitor.
SALLY ANN. What do you mean? You're supposed to be gone from this place.
AUNT JANE. Who says?
SALLY ANN. God, and the angels and the saints...

AUNT JANE *(laughs)*. Not Saint Paul.

SALLY ANN *(laughs)*. I don't suppose you'd listen to him.

AUNT JANE. I'm listening to nobody. *(She sits in the rocker, and its movement lets SALLY ANN know that she's probably sitting down.)*

SALLY ANN. You always had a mind of your own.

AUNT JANE. Seems to me there's no need to change if things are going well as they are.

SALLY ANN. But you're, well...

AUNT JANE *(chuckles)*. I guess I'm not, am I?

SALLY ANN. You're not what?

AUNT JANE. Dead.

SALLY ANN. You are to most folks.

AUNT JANE. You know most folks are blind in one way or another. Look at women's rights. We got the vote when the menfolk and even lots of the womenfolk thought we didn't have a chance. Death is the same thing. Some folks have an inkling, but they don't know 'til they're dead that they're not. *(Chuckles at the paradox.)*

SALLY ANN. I'm trying to follow you.

AUNT JANE *(laughs heartily)*. Sally Ann, this is the first time you've followed anyone.

SALLY ANN. Wait a minute, I been following you all my life.

AUNT JANE. Go on, now. You're the marcher who moves to the beat of her own drum.

SALLY ANN. Ah, but you inspired the beat. When I returned from that prissy girls' academy, you set me on my course by telling me to do just what I wanted.

AUNT JANE. Did I now?

JUST DESSERTS

SALLY ANN. You did. My father wanted me to marry Harvey and you told me I was too good for him.

AUNT JANE. Too much for him.

SALLY ANN. And then you encouraged me to go up against Uncle Billy and the legislature to try and get the wage and property laws passed.

AUNT JANE *(chuckles)*. Uncle Billy still talks about you.

SALLY ANN. Uncle Billy's dead. *(She realizes what she's said.)* I'm mighty sorry. I forgot myself.

AUNT JANE. Your eyes are opening. That's good, that's good.

SALLY ANN *(still not quite convinced)*. How is Uncle Billy? And Harvey, and Elizabeth and...

AUNT JANE. I haven't gotten around to visiting too many. There's some I'd rather not be seeing.

SALLY ANN. What's it like...being, well, where you are and all?

AUNT JANE. Not much different. I'm a mite lighter and it's easier traveling. The scenery's pretty.

SALLY ANN. Have you seen any angels or cherubim?

AUNT JANE *(chuckles)*. You'd think I'd gone to heaven.

SALLY ANN *(emphatically)*. Surely you have!

AUNT JANE. I suppose. It's bright and cheery and the folks are nice. Nothing to complain about. The food's good. I had biscuits and sausage this morning.

SALLY ANN *(suspicious)*. Are you sure you're dead?

AUNT JANE. I've been trying to tell you...that there's a mighty thin veil between you and me...and it's not all bad. Sure I can't talk to everyone I know, but you dropped by and I appreciate that. Perhaps others will stop by for a chat. Let them know, will you?

SALLY ANN. Yes, yes, I'll do that.

AUNT JANE. And you come again...as often as you like. I want to know how your running for the legislature is going. Maybe I can get Uncle Billy to whisper in a few ears. He's changed, you know. A number of us have been giving him a piece of our mind lately.

SALLY ANN. You're too much, Aunt Jane.

AUNT JANE. You go on now.

SALLY ANN. I love you, Aunt Jane.

AUNT JANE. I love you, too, Sally Ann. You'll be seeing me...

SALLY ANN *(peers closer, thinks she makes out a form).* Is that really you?

AUNT JANE. Do you think you've been talking to yourself?

SALLY ANN. No, but...

AUNT JANE. You always were a quicker learner. We'll be seeing each other sooner than later, I reckon. *(She gets up, sees the basket, picks it up and moves away, turns back and taps SALLY ANN on the shoulder.)* Thanks for removing your blinders. All it takes is a bit of horse sense.

(Startled, SALLY ANN touches her shoulder where she's been tapped. She sits in the rocker, feeling where AUNT JANE has been sitting. When she bends down, she sees that the basket is missing.)

SALLY ANN. A little horse sense. I like that. I'll use that when the menfolk start chiding me about a woman in the legislature. I'll tell them to take their blinders off. Thanks, Aunt Jane. I'm much obliged. I reckon you'll be getting lots of visitors.